THE BEST
DOGS
EVER

BOXERS
ARE THE
BEST!

Elaine Landau

Ŀ LERNER PUBLICATIONS COMPANY · MINNEAPOLIS

For Karen Lemmons

Lerner Publications Company
A division of Lerner Publishing Group, Inc.
241 First Avenue North
Minneapolis, MN 55401 U.S.A.

Website address: www.lernerbooks.com

Library of Congress Cataloging-in-Publication Data

Landau, Elaine.
    Boxers are the best! / by Elaine Landau.
        p.   cm. – (The best dogs ever)
    Includes index.
    ISBN 978-1-58013-560-3 (lib. bdg. : alk. paper)
    1. Boxer (Dog breed)–Juvenile literature. I. Title.
 SF429.B75L36 2010
    636.73–dc22   2008046787

Manufactured in the United States of America
1 2 3 4 5 6 – BP – 15 14 13 12 11 10

TABLE OF CONTENTS

CHAPTER ONE

THE CLOWN-AROUND DOG

You hear the doorbell and go to answer it. But your dog gets to the door before you. He's excited and eager to see who's there. When your guest comes in, your dog warmly welcomes him. Your pooch jumps up and plants a wet, sloppy kiss on the visitor.

Your fully grown dog has a puppy's spirit. He's always full of energy and loves being around people. You've fallen for the clown of the dog world. You have a **boxer**.

What's a Boxer Like?

Boxers are wonderful dogs. They are active and fun loving. They don't tire quickly and always want to be part of the action.

The boxer is a fine-looking dog too. Boxers are medium- to large-sized pooches. They are squarely built and solid. They have strong limbs and short, sleek coats.

BOXER NAMES

Most boxer owners feel they have the perfect dog. So they want the perfect name for their pet. Here are a few you might like.

Zinnia   CHANCE   Xavier   Rupert

Naomi

Jessica   JASPER   Buckaroo

Iris   WILLOW   Disco

Male boxers measure from 23 to 25 inches (58 to 64 centimeters) tall at the shoulder. They weigh between 65 and 80 pounds (29 and 36 kilograms). Most females are a little smaller.

Colorful Coats

Boxers come in many colors. The most common colors are fawn and brindle. Fawn dogs range from tan to a deep reddish brown. Brindle dogs are brown with black stripes.

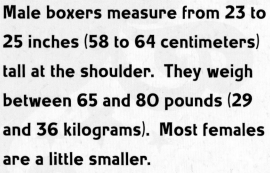

Some boxers also have white markings. These are usually on the dog's chest and feet. Such markings are known as flash. Other boxers are all white.

WHITE BOXERS

According to the American Boxer Club, about one-quarter of boxer puppies are white or mostly white. White boxers are more likely to be deaf in one or both ears. And they cannot compete in dog shows. (That's because show dogs are often used for breeding—or producing puppies. And dog breeders don't want to breed dogs that may be born with hearing problems.) But white boxers make great pets!

All boxers are fun to be with. These dogs love to clown around. Boxers often become well-loved family members. Their owners think they are the best dogs ever.

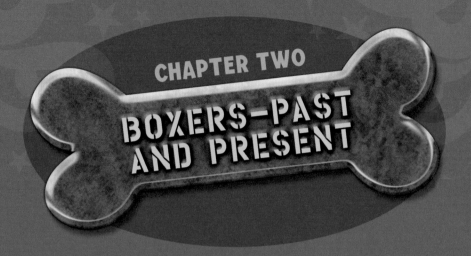

CHAPTER TWO
BOXERS—PAST AND PRESENT

Boxers are very special dogs. They date back more than one hundred years. You may think of the boxer as an all-American dog. But the boxer got its start in Germany.

Boxer Beginnings

Early on, boxers were working dogs. At first, they were used to herd livestock (animals raised on farms and ranches). They also served as guard dogs.

Later on, boxers helped the German army. During World War I (1914-1918), they served on the front lines of battle. They carried messages and helped soldiers.

BEFORE THERE WERE BOXERS

Boxers are related to dogs that lived in the sixteenth and seventeenth centuries. Those dogs helped in deer and boar hunts. They held down the prey until the hunters arrived to claim it.

Boxers' athletic skills were a big help to soldiers (left) during World War 1.

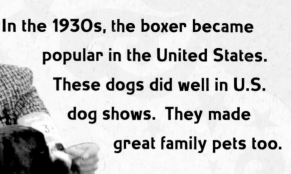

In the 1930s, the boxer became popular in the United States. These dogs did well in U.S. dog shows. They made great family pets too.

Boxers make wonderful show dogs. This boxer owner is waiting for her dog to be judged in a show.

WINNING BOXERS

Between 1947 and 1970, four boxers won Best in Show at the Westminster Kennel Club Dog Show:

- Warlord of Mazelaine (1947) Warlord's owners called him Warry at home. They fed him only top-quality meat.

- Mazelaine Zazarac Brandy (1949) This boxer broke records at the time by having sixty-one Best in Show wins from various shows.

- Bang Away of Sirrah Crest (1951) Bang Away has been called the greatest U.S. boxer ever born. He earned 121 Best in Show wins.

- Arriba's Prima Donna (1970) This super pooch has been called "a perfectly beautiful working dog."

A Working Breed

The American Kennel Club (AKC) groups dogs by breed. Some of the AKC's groups include the hound group, the toy group, and the sporting group. Boxers are in the working group.

Dogs in the working group were bred to do different jobs. All dogs in the working group are strong and smart. They are also eager to help humans.

This Afghan hound is in the hound group.

Springer spaniels, like this one, are in the sporting group.

This Yorkshire terrier belongs to the toy group.

This boxer is training to be a search and rescue dog.

Some boxers still work in modern times. They might work as therapy dogs. Therapy dogs are brought to hospitals or nursing homes. They help cheer up patients. Boxers also might work as search and rescue dogs. They find people after disasters.

Working boxers are loyal and reliable. These able dogs have proved themselves through the years.

CHAPTER THREE

A SPECIAL DOG FOR A SPECIAL OWNER

Have you been around a boxer lately? You probably loved playing with that fun pooch. Now you may want a boxer of your own.

Yet boxers need a special kind of owner. Are you that person? See how you answer the questions in the quiz on the following pages.

Boxer Quiz

1. ARE you a HiGH-eNeRgy PeRSON?

Boxers often seem to have boundless energy. What if you saw your boxer running around in circles? Would you think it was cute? Or would you be upset?

WHAT'S IN A NAME?

No one is sure where the name *boxer* comes from. Some think it comes from the way boxers move. These dogs often jump up and raise their front paws. They do this when playing or to protect themselves. It makes them look like human boxers.

2. Can you keep up with a boxer?

You should exercise your dog two to three times a day. Will you do this seven days a week?

3. Do you have time for a boxer?

Boxers are very smart dogs. They need to spend lots of time with their owners. These dogs find people fun and interesting. Beware of a bored boxer. The dog may get into mischief. It may think up its own games. These could include chewing up your shoes!

4. Are you a loner? Do you want an independent dog?

If so, don't get a boxer. Your boxer will always want to be with you.

5. Do you have the space and money for a boxer?

A boxer can be costly. These dogs need lots of dog toys. After these are chewed up, you'll have to buy more. Don't force your boxer to play with the household furnishings. It may pull down the curtains and play with them.

Boxers can get into trouble if they don't have plenty of dog toys to play with!

ALMOST HUMAN

Boxers come to know their owners well. The dogs can sense their owners' moods. Boxers learn how to put smiles on their families' faces. This can be quite comforting.

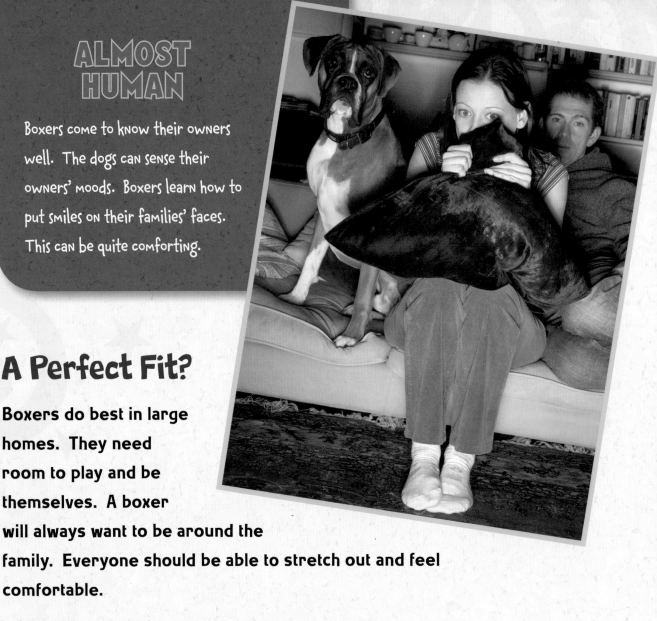

A Perfect Fit?

Boxers do best in large homes. They need room to play and be themselves. A boxer will always want to be around the family. Everyone should be able to stretch out and feel comfortable.

Boxers are not for everyone. Yet what if a boxer is a perfect fit for you and your family?

Then get set for the time of your life. Your boxer will bring you years of love and laughter!

CHAPTER FOUR

HERE COMES YOUR BOXER

Today is going to be great. You're not going on vacation or to a sleepover. Something even better is happening. You're getting a boxer!

The day your boxer comes home is special. Don't get a dog during the holiday season or on your birthday. You may be very busy with parties and people then. You need time for a new dog.

Be Ready Ahead of Time

Be prepared for your new pet. Have some doggie supplies on hand. Not sure what you'll need to welcome Fido to your family? This basic list is a great place to start:

- collar

- leash

- tags (for identification)

- dog food

- food and water bowls

- crates (one for your pet to travel in and one for it to rest in at home)

- treats (to be used in training)

- toys

CHEW, CHEW, CHEW

Puppies chew a lot. It's important to know this if you get a boxer puppy. Puppies aren't being naughty when they chew. They are teething—and teething is very painful. Chewing makes puppies' mouths feel better.

Young boxers need to have chew toys to help ease the pain of teething.

Get a Vet

Every dog needs a good veterinarian. That's a doctor who treats animals. Veterinarians are called vets for short. Take your new boxer to a vet right away. The vet will check your dog's health.

The vet will also give your boxer the shots it needs. You'll be seeing your vet again. Later on, your dog will need more shots. And you'll need to take your dog to the vet if it gets sick.

Feeding Time for Your Boxer

Feed your dog a good-quality dog food. Ask your vet which food is best.

Your dog may need different foods at different stages of its life. Don't feed your dog table scraps. Keep your boxer on a healthful diet.

Groom Your Good-Looking Dog

Boxers like to be clean. They have short coats. That means that they don't have to be bathed very often.

However, boxers still shed. Daily brushing will help get rid of old hair and dirt. It will also make your dog's coat shine.

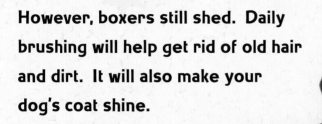

This boxer has just been groomed. Grooming makes a boxer's coat smooth and shiny.

Exercise Time!

Have fun giving your boxer the exercise it needs. Take your boxer for long walks. Play games with your dog too. Boxers love to play fetch. Many jump up to catch the ball in midair.

Do you have a fenced-in yard? That can be boxer heaven! Unleash your dog and throw a Frisbee.

BOXER HIDE-AND-SEEK

You can play hide-and-seek with your boxer. How? First, take your boxer to a fenced-in yard or dog park. (A dog park is a special park where dogs can run and play off the leash.) Then have a friend hold your boxer's leash while you run and hide somewhere nearby. Finally, have your friend release the dog and say, "Find!"

Call out to your boxer. When your dog finds you, praise your pet. After a while, your dog will be able to find you easily. You won't even have to call out!

Keep your dog leashed when away from home. Some people are afraid of large dogs. They may be frightened if they see an unleashed boxer come toward them.

Things can get even worse if the dog jumps up on someone. Your dog may just want to greet the person. However, that individual may think this is an attack.

Dog treats can be a good tool to use when you are training your boxer.

Boxers need lots of training. So you'll need lots of patience. Be prepared for this.

But boxers give a lot back in return. It's hard to find a more faithful, loving, and funny pooch. Your boxer will be your best friend.

Return the favor and treat your boxer well. You are about to become the owner of a super dog. Be the kind of owner your boxer can be proud of.

GLOSSARY

American Kennel Club (AKC): an organization that groups dogs by breed. The AKC also defines the characteristics of different breeds.

breed: a particular type of dog. Dogs of the same breed have the same body shape and general features. *Breed* can also refer to producing puppies.

brindle: brown with black stripes. Many boxers have brindle coats.

coat: a dog's fur

diet: the food your dog eats

dog park: a special park where dogs can run and play off the leash

fawn: a shade of brown. Many boxers have fawn coats.

flash: white markings on a boxer's coat

herd: to make animals move together as a group

livestock: animals raised on farms and ranches

prey: an animal that is hunted for food

search and rescue dog: a dog that finds people after disasters

shed: to lose fur

therapy dog: a dog brought to nursing homes or hospitals to comfort patients

veterinarian: a doctor who treats animals. Veterinarians are called vets for short.

working group: a group of dogs that were bred to do different types of jobs, such as guarding property, carrying messages, or pulling sleds

FOR MORE INFORMATION

Books

Brecke, Nicole, and Patricia M. Stockland. *Dogs You Can Draw*. Minneapolis: Millbrook Press, 2010. Brecke and Stockland show how to draw many different dog breeds, including the boxer.

Landau, Elaine. *Your Pet Dog*. Rev. ed. New York: Children's Press, 2007. Read this text for information on the basic care and feeding of your dog. There are also lots of tips on dog behavior.

Markle, Sandra. *Animal Heroes: True Rescue Stories*. Minneapolis: Millbrook Press, 2009. Markle tells how dogs, cats, dolphins, and other animals have saved humans from dangerous situations.

Meister, Cari. *Boxers*. Edina, MN: Abdo, 2001. This title provides interesting information for readers who want to find out more about boxers.

Stone, Lynn M. *Boxers*. Vero Beach, FL: Rourke Publishing, 2005. You'll see how boxers work, eat, and play in this book. You'll also learn more about boxer history.

Websites

American Kennel Club

http://www.akc.org

Visit this website to find a complete listing of AKC-registered dog breeds, including the boxer. The site also features fun printable activities for kids.

ASPCA Animaland

http://www.aspca.org/site/PageServer?pagename=kids_pc_home

Check out this page for helpful hints on caring for a dog and other pets.

Index

Quotation Acknowledgments

P. 11, Katherine Nicholas, quoted in Christina Ghimenti, "Arriba Boxers: Page 1," *PawPrint Boxers*, n.d., http://www.angelfire.com/ca2/pawprintboxers/arriba.html (November 13, 2008).

Photo Acknowledgments

The images in this book are used with the permission of: © iofoto/snapvillage.com, p. 4; © Margo Harrison/Shutterstock Images, p. 5; © david woodberry Pure Eye Photo/Shutterstock Images, p. 6 (left); © Eric IsseLee/Shutterstock Images, pp. 6 (right); © Rachel Watson/Taxi/Getty Images, p. 7 (top); © Justin-Julius Santos/Getty Images, p. 7 (bottom); © Sulus-Veer/CORBIS, p. 8; © Drazen Vukelic/Shutterstock Images, p. 9; © Haeckel Brothers/FPG/Hulton Archive/Getty Images, p. 10 (top); © Biosphoto/Klein J.-L. & Hubert M.-L./Peter Arnold, Inc., pp. 10 (bottom), 19, 21 (left), 29; © Jonathan Littlejohn/Alamy.com. p. 11; © isselee/Dreamstime.com, p. 12 (left); © Jose Louis Palaez, Inc./Blend Images/Getty Images, p. 12 (center); © istockphoto.com/Eric Isselee, p. 12 (right); © JAY DIRECTO/Getty Images, p. 13 (top); © WILDLIFE/Peter Arnold, Inc., p. 13 (bottom); © Patrick Sheandell O'Carroll/Getty Images, p. 14; © iStockphoto.com/ludovic rhodes, p. 15; © iStockphoto.com/Guillermo Perales Gonzalez, p. 16 (left); © Tad Denson/Shutterstock Images, p. 16 (right); © Jacobs Stock Photography/Getty Images, p. 17 (inset); © Marcelo Santos/Getty Images, p. 17 (main); © Francine Fleischer/Flirt/CORBIS, p. 18; © Larry Gatz/Photographer's Choice/Getty Images, pp. 19 (right), 20 (bottom); © Jo Sax/Taxi/Getty Images, p. 20 (top); © DTP/Digital Vision/Getty Images, p. 22; © Margaret Miller/Photo Researchers, Inc., p. 23; © Juniors Bildarchiv/F215/Alamy, p. 24; © DK Limited/CORBIS, p. 25 (main); © Sander Jurkiewicz/Alamy, p. 25 (bottom); © George Lee/Shutterstock Images, p. 26 (left); © Biosphoto/Thiriet Claudius/Peter Arnold, Inc., p. 26 (main); © Biosphoto/Digoit Olivier/Peter Arnold, Inc., p. 27; © Stana/Shutterstock Images, p. 28 (bottom); © Dennis Kleiman/UpperCut images/Getty Images, p. 28 (top).

Front cover: © Photodisc/Getty Images; back cover © iofoto/snapvillage.com.